M

KT-404-406

Note to Parents and Teachers

The READING ABOUT: STARTERS series introduces key science vocabulary to young children while encouraging them to discover and understand the world around them. The series works as a set of graded readers in three levels.

LEVEL 2: BEGIN TO READ ALONE follows guidelines set out in the National Curriculum for Year 2 in schools. These books can be read alone or as part of ' group reading. Each book has three sections:

ROYAL BOation pages that introduce key words. These key words appear in bold for
ognition on pages where the related science concepts are explained.
ely story that recalls this vocabulary and encourages children to use these
when they talk and write.
uiz and index ask children to look back and recall what they have read.

stions for Further Investigation

AT'S INSIDE ME? explains key concepts about LIFE PROCESSES. Here are some
estions for further discussion linked to the questions on the information spreads:

What living things do you see? Remind children that plants as well as animals are
g things, even though they move so slowly it is hard to see their movements.

What bones can you feel under your skin? You could introduce other names of
es that are easy to find, such as the pelvis, shin bone and elbow (funny) bone.

11 *How can you make your muscles stronger?* Ask children to think about which
ds of exercise work which parts of their body, e.g. swimming, dancing, cycling.

13 *Why do you breathe slower when you are asleep?* Explain how body slows itself
wn when it sleeps so it can rest. However, brain is still very active, which is why we
ve dreams, like almost all mammals (so dogs and cats have dreams too)!

15 *When does your heart beat faster?* Ask children to feel their pulse before and after
exercise. Could also mention that our heart beats faster when we are excited or scared.

p. 17 *Why do you think your brain is inside your skull?* Your skull protects your brain.
Our brain is so important that often we must protect it in other ways, e.g. cycling helmet.

19 *How do senses warn you about danger?* Ask children which senses warn people
nd animals about different dangers: e.g. fire/hot things, heights, cars, predators etc.

23 *How else can you help your body to feel better?* Ask children to think about what
akes them feel good, e.g. having fun, resting, keeping warm/cool in winter/summer.

DVISORY TEAM

Educational Consultant
Andrea Bright – Science Co-ordinator, Trafalgar Junior School, Twickenham

Literacy Consultant
Jackie Holderness – former Senior Lecturer in Primary Education, Westminster Institute, Oxford Brookes University

Series Consultants
Anne Fussell – Early Years Teacher and University Tutor, Westminster Institute, Oxford Brookes University

David Fussell – C.Chem., FRSC

JN

CONTENTS

4   animal, alive, living

6   food, energy, stomach

8   bone, skeleton, joints

10 move, muscle, exercise

12 lung, breathe, oxygen

14 heart, pump, blood, vessel

16 brain, think

18 senses

20 baby, grow

22 ill, medicine, healthy

24 **Story: A Day at the Beach**
Sun, swimming & sandcastles!

31 Quiz

32 Index

PAPERBACK EDITION PRINTED 2007
© Aladdin Books Ltd 2005

Designed and produced by
Aladdin Books Ltd
2/3 Fitzroy Mews
London W1T 6DF

First published in 2005
in Great Britain by
Franklin Watts
338 Euston Road
London NW1 3BH

Franklin Watts Australia
Hachette Children's Books
Level 17/207 Kent Street
Sydney NSW 2000

A catalogue record for this book is available from the British Library.
Dewey Classification: 612
ISBN 978 07496 7528 8

Printed in Malaysia

All rights reserved

Editor: Jim Pipe

Design: Flick, Book Design and Graphics

Thanks to: The pupils of Trafalgar Infants School, Twickenham • Lynne Thompson • The pupils and teachers of Trafalgar Junior School, Twickenham and St. Nicholas C.E. Infant School, Wallingford.

Photocredits:
l-left, r-right, b-bottom, t-top, c-centre, m-middle
Cover tr, tm & tl, 2ml, 4ml, 11tr, 16c, 31tr — Brand X Pictures. Cover b, 6br, 8mr, 10bl, 12 both, 14 both, 22tl, 23b, 31tr — Marc Arundale/ Select Pictures. 2tl, 3, 4br, 10mr, 11l, 17b, 19br & ml, 21bl, 22tr, 29, 31mr, 31bl, 31br — Comstock. 2bl, 13, 15b, 18 both, 24br, 26br, 31bc — Digital Vision. 5t, 9t, 27mr, 28tr — Eyewire (Photodisc). 5b, 8r, 21tr, 25 all, 28ml, 32 — Ingram Publishing. 6 all (except 6br) — Stockbyte. 7, 17tr — Select Pictures. 9br, 15tr — Jim Pipe. 19tr — PBD. 21t, 22b, 27tl, 30mr — Corbis. 21br, 24tr — Ken Hammond/USDA. 24ml, 26t — Photodisc. 28br — Corel.

Starters LIFE PROCESSES

What's Inside Me?

By Sally Hewitt

Aladdin/Watts
London • Sydney

Plants and **animals** are **alive**.
You are a kind of **animal** so you are **alive**.

Plants and **animals** are **living** things.
All **living** things do the same things.

- They need food and water.

- They move.

- They breathe air in and out.

• **Living** things can sense the world around them.

• They grow and they make new life like themselves.

• Look around you. What living things can you see?

Food gives you **energy**. Different **foods** help to keep you strong and healthy.

Eggs, nuts, meat

Wheat bread, pasta

Cheese, milk

Vegetables, fruit

Eat some of these different kinds of **food** every day. Your body needs lots of water every day, too!

6

You chew your **food**. You swallow it.
The **food** goes into your **stomach**.
Your **stomach** mashes
it up.

Your blood carries
goodness from the
food all around
your body.

Stomach

You get
rid of waste
that you don't
need when you go
to the bathroom.

• Follow food with your finger on its journey through
the boy's body. Then imagine it inside your body.

7

Your **bones** make a frame for your body called a **skeleton**.

Your **skeleton** protects the soft parts inside your body.

Without a **skeleton** your body would have no shape!

Skull

Ribs

Arm bones

Leg bones

You can feel strong bones under your skin.

8

Your arms and legs bend at your elbows and knees.

Elbows and knees are called **joints** because they are where your **bones join** together.

Your wrists, ankles, and neck are **joints**, too.

• What bones can you feel under your skin?

You can **move** because you have **muscles** all over your body.

You have small **muscles** in your face. Feel them pull your skin when you smile.

You have big **muscles** in your back, legs, and arms.

Big muscles pull your bones when you move.

Face muscles

Your **muscles** work hard when you run and jump.

Exercise keeps **muscles** strong and healthy.

Arm muscles

Stand on tiptoe. Feel the **muscle** in the back of your leg bulge.

Dancers have strong **muscles** in their legs.

• How can you make your muscles stronger?

Behind your ribs are your two **lungs**.
You **breathe** air with your **lungs**
all day and all night.

**Feeling
your lungs**

Feel your **lungs** fill with
fresh air as you **breathe**
in. Feel them empty as
you **breathe** out.

Stale air from
your lungs fills
a balloon when
you blow it up.

12

You need **oxygen** from the air to stay alive. So you must **breathe** all the time.

When you exercise, your body needs more **oxygen**.
Your lungs must work hard.

After exercise you **breathe** in and out very fast.

Exercise

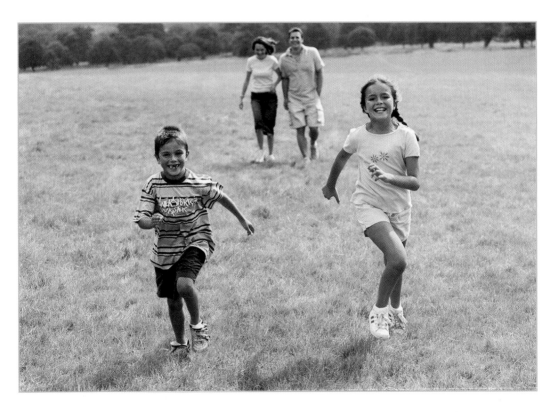

• Why do you breathe slower when you are asleep?

Your **heart** is also behind your ribs. It is a strong muscle that **pumps blood** all around your body.

You can hear your **heart pumping** in your chest. This is called your heartbeat.

Feel your pulse beat in your wrist. It's your heartbeat!

Listening to heart

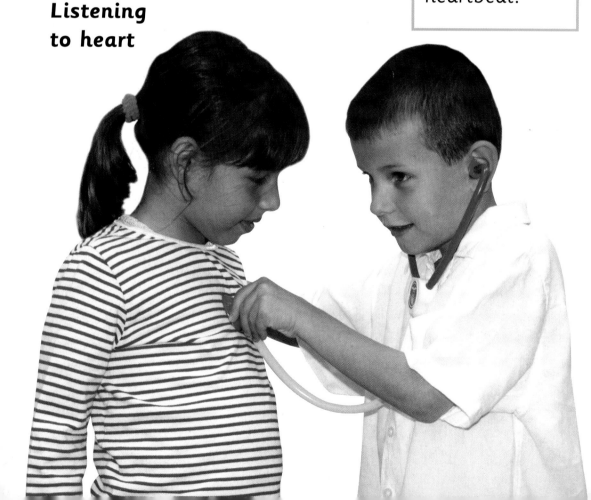

Blood flows around your body through tubes called **blood vessels**.

When you have a cut, you see your **blood**. The **blood** dries into a scab. Your skin gets better below it.

Cut

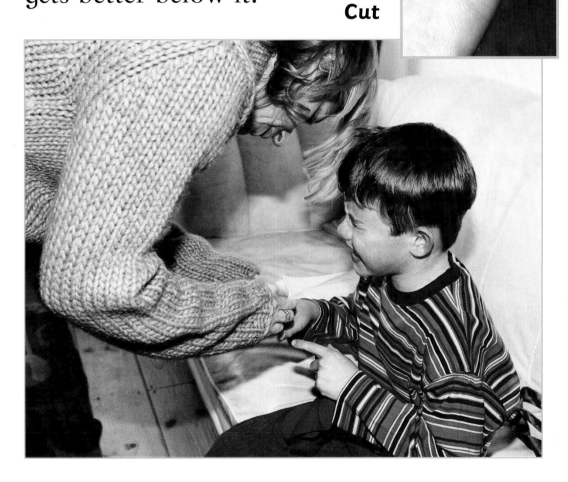

• When does your heart beat faster?

You have a **brain** that controls everything you do.

All animals have **brains**. But only humans can talk, read, and write.

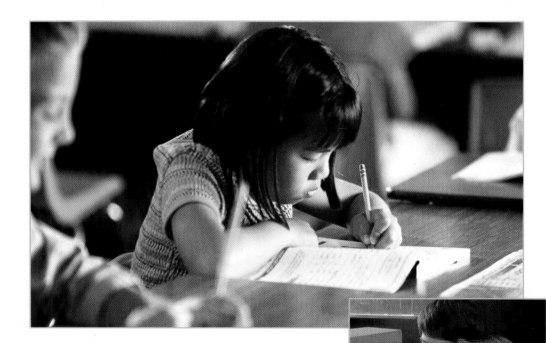

You **think** with your **brain**.

It is more powerful than any computer.

Computer

16

Your **brain** is in your head.
It sends messages to the
rest of your body.

Your **brain** tells the rest of
your body what to do.

Your brain is
soft, like a
gray, wrinkly
sponge.

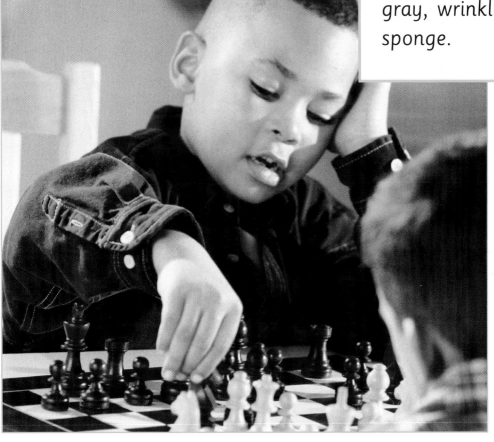

• Why do you think your brain is inside your skull?

Your **senses** tell you what is going on around you.

You taste with your tongue and smell with your nose.

You see with your eyes and hear with your ears. You feel with your skin.

Your **senses** also warn you about danger!

Your eyes, ears, nose, tongue, and skin are connected to your brain.

They send messages back to your brain. Your brain tells you what you are **sensing**.

Your senses keep you safe. You look and listen for traffic before you cross the road.

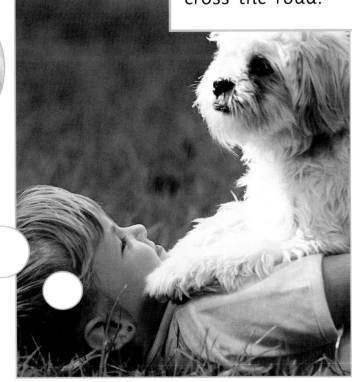

Seeing a dog

• How do your senses warn you about danger?

A human **baby grows** inside its mother. After nine months it is ready to be born.

A **baby** drinks its mother's milk.

It needs to be looked after all the time.

20

Baby

A **baby grows** into a child.
A child **grows** into a teenager.
A teenager **grows** into
an adult.

When you
become an
adult you will
stop **growing**.

But you won't
stop changing
and learning
new things!

• What clues tell you how old someone is?

Tiny germs can give you a cold. Use a hankie if you sneeze so no one else catches the germs.

When you feel **ill**, you go to the doctor. The doctor takes your temperature and feels your pulse.

You may need **medicine** to help you get better.

If you need an operation, you may go to the hospital.

You can help yourself stay **healthy**.

You can eat good food, drink lots of water, and get plenty of exercise and sleep.

• How *else* can you help your body to feel better?

A DAY AT THE BEACH

Look out for words about your **body**.

Poppy and Adam were very excited. They were going to the beach.

"Are you too old to come too, Grandpa?" asked Adam.

Grandpa laughed. "My **bones** are a bit creaky. The sea will do them good!" he said.

"Can **baby** Jake swim with us?" asked Poppy.
"Not until he **grows** a bit," said Mom.
"But he'll love the soft sand."

"I'll make the picnic," said Mom.
"We'll need lots of **food** and plenty of drinks."

"I can't find my swimsuit!" said Adam.
"**Think** hard," said Mom. "I remember!" said Adam. "It's in my sports bag."

"I'll get the pails and shovels," said Poppy.

"Don't forget hats and sunscreen to protect your skin," said Dad. "And sunglasses, too!"

25

When they got there, the sun was shining.

"The sea makes you feel **alive**!" said Grandpa.
"I can feel the sand in my toes!" said Mom.
"I can taste the salty sea air!" said Poppy.
"I can hear the waves!" said Dad.

"I'll take a picture,"
said Grandpa.

"Smile, everyone!"

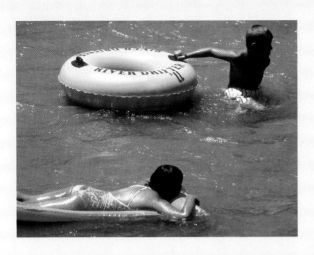

"Let's go for a swim," said Dad.

"Look, your friends are already in the water."

"Can we blow up my ring?" asked Poppy.
"Yes," said Dad, "But you'll need strong **lungs**."

"Watch me swim underwater!" said Adam.
"But you can't **breathe** underwater!" said Poppy.
"I'll hold my **breath**," said Adam.

Adam and Dad went for a swim. Poppy played with her ring in the shallow water.

27

After their swim, Poppy and
Adam played with Lucy.

"Don't throw the ball hard,
Adam," said Lucy. "You've
got bigger **muscles** than me!"

"All this **exercise** is making
me tired!" said Poppy.

"I'm hungry, too!" said Adam.
"My **stomach** is rumbling!"

"Time for a rest and some food," said Mom.
"It will give you more **energy**."

After the picnic,
Grandpa and **baby**
Jake went to sleep
in the shade.

Adam and Poppy built a sandcastle
with their friends.

When Grandpa woke up, he said, "My **joints**
feel stiff. Come on, children, let's go for a walk!"

Adam, Poppy, and Grandpa walked a long
way down the beach. Then Grandpa said,
"It's late. We should go back."

"Let's race back to the others!" shouted Adam.

When they arrived they were out of **breath.**
Poppy could feel her **heart pumping** fast.

"Where's our sandcastle?" asked Poppy.
"Did it **move**?"

"Look!" said Adam.
"The tide came in. We're
standing on it!"

"Let's use our **brains** next
time and build one farther
from the sea!" laughed Poppy.

Think about an activity you enjoy, such as
going swimming. Can you write a list of the
parts of your body you might use? Or draw
pictures to show how your body works.

If I cut
myself,
the blood
will dry
into a scab.

I have big
muscles in
my arms.
I can swing
on the bars.

QUIZ

How can you keep your
muscles strong and healthy?

Answer on page 11

What does
your **heart** do?

Answer on page 14

What parts of your body
sense the world around you?

Answer on page 18-19

Children are living things.
What are these children doing?
What else can living things do?

Have you read this book? Well done! Do you remember these words? Look back and find out.

INDEX

A
alive 4
animal 4

B
baby 20
blood 14
bone 8
brain 16
breathe 12

E
energy 6
exercise 10

F
food 6

G
grow 20

H
healthy 22
heart 14

I
ill 22

J
joints 8

L
living 4
lung 12

M
medicine 22
move 10
muscle 10

O
oxygen 12

P
pump 14

S
senses 18
skeleton 8
stomach 6

T
think 16

V
vessel 14